How To Rehearse In Order To Give The Perfect Speech

How to effectively rehearse your next speech so that your message will be remembered forever!

"Practical, proven techniques that will help you to make your next speech a success"

Dr. Jim Anderson

Published by:
Blue Elephant Consulting
Tampa, Florida

Copyright © 2013 by Dr. Jim Anderson

All rights reserved. No part of this book may be reproduced of transmitted in any form or by any means, electronic or mechanical, including photocopying, recording or by any information storage and retrieval system without written permission of the publisher, except for inclusion of brief quotations in a review.

Printed in the United States of America

Library of Congress Control Number: 2013956585

ISBN-13: 978-1494321987
ISBN-10: 149432198X

Warning – Disclaimer

The purpose of this book is to educate and entertain. This book does not promise or guarantee that anyone following the ideas, tips, suggestions, techniques or strategies will be hired. It is the discretion of employers if you will or will not be hired. The author, publisher and distributor(s) shall have neither liability nor responsibility to anyone with respect to any loss or damage caused, or alleged to be caused, directly or indirectly by the information contained in this book.

Recent Books By The Author

Product Management

- How To Have A Successful Product Manager Career: The Things That You Need To Be Doing TODAY In Order To Have A Successful Product Manager Career

- Product Manager Product Success: How to keep your product on track and make it become a success

- Communication Skills For Product Managers: The Communication Skills That Product Managers Need To Know How To Use In Order To Have A Successful Product

Public Speaking

- Secrets To Planning The Perfect Speech

- Secrets To Organizing The Perfect Speech: How to organize the best speech of your life!

- Secrets To Creating The Perfect Speech: How to create a speech that will make your message be remembered forever!

CIO Skills

- CIO Business Skills: How CIOs can work effectively with the rest of the company!

- Managing Your CIO Career: Steps That CIOs Have To Take In Order To Have A Long And Successful Career

- CIO Communication Skills Secrets: Tips And Techniques For CIOs To Use In Order To Become Better Communicators

IT Manager

- IT Manager Budgeting Skills

- IT Manager Career Secrets: Tips And Techniques That IT Managers Can Use In Order To Have A Successful Career

- Secrets Of Effective Leadership For IT Managers : Tips And Techniques That IT Managers Can Use In Order To Develop Leadership Skills

Negotiating

- Preparing For Your Next Negotiation: What You Need To Do BEFORE A Negotiation Starts In Order To Get The Best Possible Deal

- How To Open Your Next Negotiation: How To Start A Negotiation In Order To Get The Best Possible Outcome

- Learn How To Argue In Your Next Negotiation: How To Develop The Skill Of Effective Arguing In A Negotiation In Order To Get The Best Possible Outcome

Note: See a complete list of books by Dr. Jim Anderson at the back of this book

Acknowledgements

Any book like this one is the result of years of real-world work experience. In my over 25 years of working for 7 different firms, I have met countless fantastic people and I've been mentored by some truly exceptional ones. Although I've probably forgotten some of the people who made me the person that I am today, here is my attempt to finally give them the recognition that they so truly deserve:

- Thomas P. Anderson
- Art Puett
- Bobbi Marshall
- Bob Boggs

Dr. Jim Anderson

This book is dedicated to my wife Lori. None of this would have been possible without her love and support.

Thanks for the best 21 years of my life (so far)...!

Table Of Contents

JUST HOW IMPORTANT IS REHEARSING YOUR NEXT SPEECH?..........8

ABOUT THE AUTHOR...10

CHAPTER 1: A FEW NOTES ABOUT NOTES..15

CHAPTER 2: HOW TO USE THE 150" HDTV THAT LIVES IN YOUR HEAD 19

CHAPTER 3: HOW TO USE YOUR MENTAL TV TO MEMORIZE A SPEECH (OR ANYTHING)..23

CHAPTER 4: PRESENTATION PRACTICE: HOW MUCH IS ENOUGH? ...29

CHAPTER 5: LIGHTS, CAMERA, TV PRESENTATION? 4 TIPS FOR SPEAKING ON TELEVISION...33

CHAPTER 6: ARE YOU ACTING LIKE A PRESENTER?...........................37

CHAPTER 7: WHY DON'T YOU ACT LIKE A PRESENTER DURING YOUR PRESENTATION?...41

CHAPTER 8: THE PRESENTER SUPER MEMORY SYSTEM – AN OVERVIEW 44

CHAPTER 9: THE PRESENTER SUPER MEMORY SYSTEM – THE DETAILS 47

CHAPTER 10: HEY SPEAKER – IT'S TOOL TIME! 50

CHAPTER 11: YOUR PRESENTATION VOICE: IS THAT REALLY ME?.....53

CHAPTER 12: THIS SPEECH WILL BE DELIVERED IN (GOOD) ENGLISH 56

Just How Important Is Rehearsing Your Next Speech?

Every time we are asked to give a speech, we feel a sense of nervous energy flow through our body. We think "I hope that this turns out well." We would give anything to be able to control the future and make this our best speech ever. Well, I've got some good news for you: you are in control and you can make that happen.

The secret to delivering a great speech is to know how to rehearse your speech. The reason that so many of us don't bother with rehearsing our speeches is for the simple fact that it takes time – who ever has enough of that?

The sad truth is that just how effective our next speech is lies in our own hands. Take the time to not only rehearse your speech, but rehearse it the correct way and then when it's time to give your speech, you'll be ready.

A big part of why we rehearse our speeches is because we want to remember what we're going to be saying. There are a lot of different ways to go about doing this – some easy, some hard. I think that I've discovered a way that will make this task easy for every speaker.

Not every speech is the same. When we are asked to speak on Television, as more and more of us are, the rules are very different. As long as we know what the rules are, we can come away from this opportunity having been very successful.

Rehearsing your speech consists of so much more than just repeating your speech over and over again. Each rehearsal gives you an opportunity to work on your acting skills, your voice, and how you build the sentences that you'll be using in your speech.

In this book all of the secrets to getting the most out of the time that you spend rehearsing for your speech will be shared. We'll cover how to memorize your speech, how to deliver it, and how you can control what you sound like. After you have read this book, you'll be able to rehearse for you next speech knowing that your time is being spent wisely.

For more information on what it takes to be a great public speaker, check out my blog, The Accidental Communicator, at:

www.TheAccidentalCommunicator.com

Good luck!

- Dr. Jim Anderson

About The Author

I must confess that I never set out to be a public speaker. When I went to school, I studied Computer Science and thought that I'd get a nice job programming and that would be that. Well, at least part of that plan worked out!

My first job was working for Boeing on their F/A-18 fighter jet program. I spent my days programming fighter jet software in assembly language and I loved it. The U.S. government decided to save some money and went looking for other countries to sell this plane to. This put me into an unfamiliar role: I started to meet with foreign military officials and I ended up having to give speeches in order to explain what my product did.

Time moved on and so did I. I found myself working for Siemens, the big German telecommunications company. They were making phone switches and selling them to the seven U.S. phone companies. The problem was that the switches were too complicated. Customers couldn't tell the difference between one complicated phone switch from another complicated phone switch. Once again I found myself standing in front of the room giving speeches in order to explain what these complicated machines did and why ours were better than anyone else's.

I've spent over 25 years working as a product manager for both big companies and startups. This has given me an opportunity to do many, many presentations for customers, at conferences, and everywhere in-between.

I now live in Tampa Florida where I spend my time managing my consulting business, Blue Elephant Consulting, teaching college courses at the University of South Florida, and traveling to work with companies like yours to share the knowledge that I have about how to create and deliver powerful and effective speeches.

I'm always available to answer questions and I can be reached at:

Dr. Jim Anderson
Blue Elephant Consulting
Email: jim@BlueElephantConsulting.com
Facebook: http://goo.gl/1TVoK
Web: **www.BlueElephantConsulting.com**

"Unforgettable communication skills that will set your ideas free…"

Create Speeches That Motivate Your Audiences And Get Your Message Heard!

Dr. Jim Anderson is available to provide training and coaching on the topics that are the most important to people who have to speak in public: how can I create a speech that people want to hear and how can I deliver in a way that will allow me to connect with my audience and get my point across to them?

Dr. Anderson believes that in order to both learn and remember what he says, speakers need to laugh. Each one of his speeches is full of fun and humor so that what he says "sticks" with everyone.

Dr. Anderson's Public Speaking Training Includes:

1. How to plan your next speech: pick your purpose and understand your audience.
2. What's the best way to get PowerPoint and Keynote to work with you, not against you?
3. What do you need to do when you are presenting in order to truly connect with your audience?

Dr. Jim Anderson presents over 100 speeches per year. To invite Dr. Anderson to speak at your event, contact him at:

Phone: 813-418-6970 or
Email: jim@BlueElephantConsulting.com

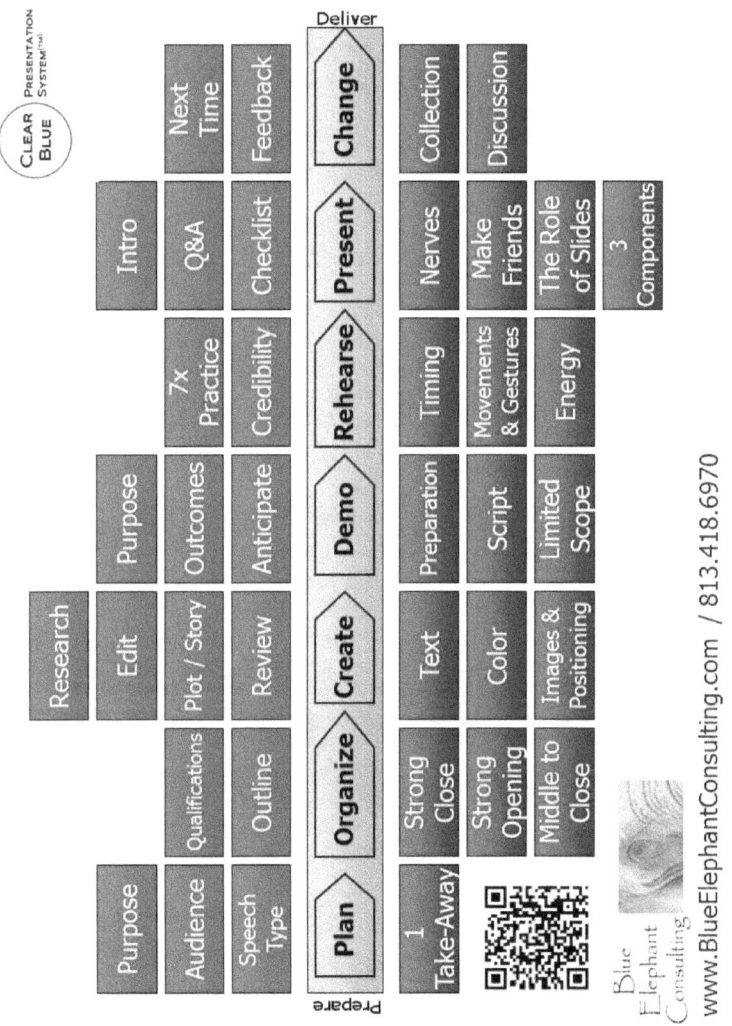

Blue Elephant Consulting has created the **Clear Blue™** presentation system for creating and delivering powerful and memorable presentations. The contents of this book are based on lessons learned during the development of the Clear Blue system. Contact Blue Elephant Consulting to learn more about the Clear Blue presentation system.

Chapter 1

A Few Notes About Notes

Chapter 1: A Few Notes About Notes

How can you tell when you are going to be sitting through an absolutely terrible speech? There are a lot of ways, but one sure fire sign is when you see the presenter approaching the podium with a big handful of notes that seem to be exploding from whatever he/she has them barely contained in.

As the speaker takes the next five minutes to find the start of their notes, everyone in the audience has a chance to sit and squirm because we all know what's coming next – complete boredom! What's interesting is that it's often not the speaker's fault, but rather the fault of the notes that they are using.

If the job of every speaker is to connect with their audience, then notes sure seem to be a big brick wall that stands in the way of accomplishing that goal. Why is this?

Why do people who speak using notes have such a hard time connecting with their audience? The answer, it turns out, is actually pretty simple.

When you are standing in front of a live audience and every so often you pause to look down at notes, this really screws up your brain. I mean think about it, there you are having this wonderful conversation with your audience when all of a sudden you stop the conversation, look down and start to read.

Then you look back up and while your brain is trying to process what you've just read, your mouth opens up and tries to jump right back in where you had left off. If you look down frequently, you are almost certain to screw up your speech eventually.

Having said all of this, it may come as somewhat of a surprise to you that I'm going to tell you that I'm actually a big fan of speaker's notes. Why you ask?

I have seem too many speeches where the speaker was half way through and then for some unknown reason just lost it. If the speaker didn't have notes, then there was this very long, painful, silence in which the speaker completely shut out the audience while he/she desperately tried to remember both where they were and what came next. Ouch!

So I fully believe that every speaker should have a nice outline of their speech with them and lay it on the podium as a sort of insurance policy. If everything goes well, then hopefully the speaker will never have to refer to it. However, in case there is a perfect storm, then there is a lifeboat ready and waiting for the speaker.

Dr. Steve Reagles has a couple of suggestions: oral writing and oral practice (don't laugh). When he talks about oral writing he's really suggesting that you keep four points in mind:

1. **Keep it simple**: make it so that your audience can easily picture what you are talking about.

2. **Tell 'em What You're Talking About**: make sure that you tell your audience what your point is – don't make them guess based on the material that you've presented.

3. **Make It Memorable**: Be sure to lay in rich details and interesting examples so that your audience can remember what you talked about.

4. **Tie It Up!**: Make sure that you have ideas that run throughout your entire speech that you can use to tie

various sections together and to make a seamless whole.

After you have that taken care of, Dr. Reagles suggests that you practice, practice, practice. He makes the good point that it's through practice that we are able to lift the words that we write in an outline up and turn them into a verbal performance.

Chapter 2

How To Use The 150" HDTV That Lives In Your Head

Chapter 2: How To Use The 150" HDTV That Lives In Your Head

Have you seen those giant flat screen TVs that they are selling these days down at Best Buy stores? They are HUGE! In fact, they are so large and so bright that you'd almost have to go next door in order to properly watch them if you bought one.

Of course buying one is still an issue – you're looking at $2,000 – $4,000 for the just the TV and then twice as much for installation, surround sound, Blue-Ray DVD, etc. So what does all of this home theater talk have to do with how we communicate?

Plenty – it turns out that you already have one of these giant TVs in your head and it's just sitting there waiting to be turned on in order to help you next time you have a presentation to give.

We've talked about how dangerous it can be to show up to give a presentation with a big stack of notes. However, we really never discussed what else you could do to make sure that you were able to deliver your presentation in the proper order and not leave out any of the important information.

In order to answer this question, I need you to come with me back about 2,500 years ago or so to ancient Greece. Back in these days presentations were given without the benefit of PowerPoint and in fact, there wasn't really any good way to create a bunch of notes.

Orators gave hour long (or longer) speeches and had to get each and every word right every time they gave the same speech. How the heck did they do that?

The answer can be found in one word: memorization. Now I'm just a bit cautious using this word because it's too easy to take it the wrong way.

We've all probably seen speakers who have written out speeches word-for-word, practiced them over and over, and then tried to deliver them without using any notes. Whereas this is quite the impressive feat, the results are almost always less than spectacular – they struggle so hard to recall the next word that we end up feeling worn out for them by the time that they are done presenting. The fancy name for the wrong way to memorize things is rote learning.

How about if we use a different way of memorizing your speech? The way that I'm going to present to you will allow you to use that big 150" HDTV in your head and just sit back and watch your speech play out for you in full surround sound as you simply tell your audience what you are seeing. What could be easier? This approach is called the loci method.

In order to memorize your speech using the loci method, you need to do three things:

1. Break the speech up into a sequence of steps. These steps need to be as small as you can make them and they need to be placed in a sequential order: start, middle, and end.

2. You need to associate an image AND an action with each step of your speech. The wilder and more outrageous the image/action is the easier that step is going to be to remember.

3. Finally, you need to "place" all of your steps someplace where you will be able to find them. If your speech was short and only had 10 steps, then I'd suggest that you visualize yourself "placing"

them on your body: toes, ankles, knees, shins, hips, butt, back, shoulders, neck, and head. If you have more steps, then I'd use some place that you know very well: your home is a great place to start. Think of your bedroom and "place" each step on things that are currently in your bedroom.

Chapter 3

How To Use Your Mental TV To Memorize A Speech (or Anything)

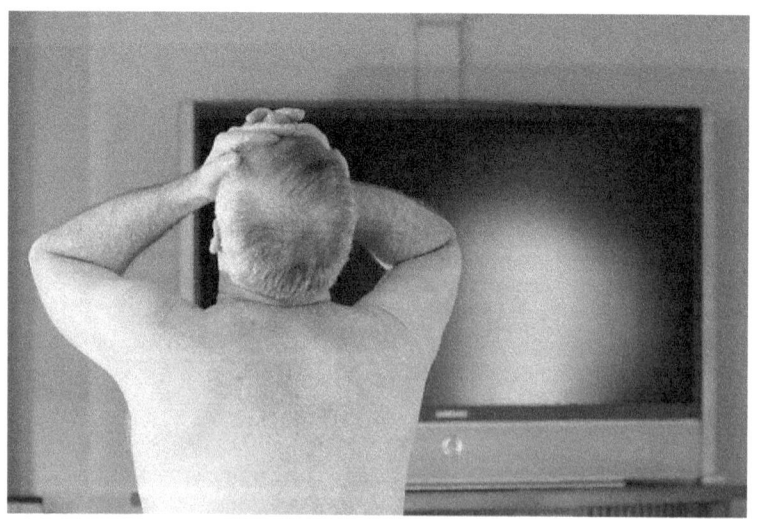

Chapter 3: How To Use Your Mental TV To Memorize A Speech (or Anything)

Back when I was in school, I was taking mainly technical courses and I got to be pretty good at them. The routine was pretty much the same for each class: learn the formula, work some problems to practice using the formula, take a test and show that you know how to use the formula.

The same thing went for my Computer Science classes except that instead of formulas, we were dealing with computer languages. You can well imagine how surprised and unprepared I was when I had to take some business courses: there were no formulas!

Instead, there was a great deal of "facts" that needed to be memorized and then dumped back out of your head while you were taking a test. My friends who were in Business School had become very good at this type of memorize / dump routine; however, I was basically clueless.

Eventually I found a way to get all of that information to stick in my brain. What was even better was that, unlike my friends, it would remain there long after the test / final exam had come and gone. I had truly found a way to memorize my material.

This is exactly the skill that you need when you have an opportunity to give a speech. You need to memorize your speech in such a way that it comes back to you quickly and easily each and every time that you need to give the speech without the need for any notes.

In fact, if you could find a way to get your speech to play out on that big TV in your head, then all you would have to do is watch it and tell your audience what you were seeing. Sounds like an impossible dream? It's not and I'm going to show you how to do it.

First, let's start with just a little bit of medical knowledge so that you understand why this technique works. Based on years of research, Doctors believe that the part of the human brain that is responsible for our memories is the part that is called the hippocampus.

Here's the important part: if this part of the brain is stimulated sufficiently, then we will remember what stimulated it. We are all very visually based beings.

This means that our memories are made up of images – sorta like a big stack of photographs. If you can visualize something, then it suddenly becomes much easier to remember it.

That's why long phone numbers can be hard to memorize (no good picture) and why what a fancy new car looks like (it's all about looks) can be easy to recall even if you've only see it once.

In order to memorize your speech, you need to do three things:

1. Break the speech up into a sequence of steps. These steps need to be as small as you can make them and they need to be placed in a sequential order: start, middle, and end.

2. You need to associate an image AND an action with each step of your speech. The wilder and more outrageous the image/action is the easier that step is going to be to remember.

3. Finally, you need to "place" all of your steps someplace where you will be able to find them. If your speech was short and only had 10 steps, then I'd suggest that you

visualize yourself "placing" them on your body: toes, ankles, knees, shins, hips, butt, back, shoulders, neck, and head. If you have more steps, then I'd use some place that you know very well: your home is a great place to start. Think of your bedroom and "place" each step on things that are currently in your bedroom.

Now comes the fun part. In order to memorize your speech, what you are really going to be doing is running thorough your list and recalling the images/actions that you have stored in each location.

The key to success is that you'll need to recall each step in proper sequential order and you'll be need to be able to do it with little or no effort. How about an example to make this all seem just a little bit more real?

Let's say that you were asked to give a presentation on your company's new 401k program (how boring would that be?)

Here are the key points that you need to cover in your speech: everyone is automatically enrolled upon joining the company, you can un-enroll, the company will match the first 5% that you contribute, if you leave the company you can take your 401k with you, and you can borrow against your 401k in special circumstances. Yawn! Now let's do some work to memorize this speech:

1. Break it into steps:

    - everyone is automatically enrolled upon joining the company,

    - you can un-enroll,

- the company will match the first 5% that you contribute,

- if you leave the company you can take your 401k with you,

- you can borrow against your 401k in special circumstances.

2. Now create pictures / actions for each step (sorry, these pictures/actions work for me – results may vary for you):

    - I see an assembly line of new employees moving along past a machine that stamps "401k" on everyone's forehead. The stamp hits them with a big "smack" sound and leaves a big red mark.

    - I see some new employees on the assembly line, after they have been stamped, reaching up and peeling off a piece of clear tape that covered their forehead and, because it got stamped and not their actual forehead, they can just throw it away and they are not labeled as "401k" like everyone else

    - I see the employees on the assembly line one-by-one stopping at a table where an accountant wearing a green visor and sitting at a plain wooden table sits. Each employee starts to lay down $1 bills on the table and as he does so, the accountant lays another $1 bill down on the table right by the employee's bill. However, once the employee lays down his 6th $1 bill, the accountant stops laying his money down. The employee scoops up all of the money and gets back on the assembly line.

- I see some employees jumping off of the assembly line holding big piles of cash and vanishing through a hole in the floor that has a big flashing "EXIT" sign beside it.

- I see an employee jumping off of the assembly line and running towards a house that is fully on fire. The employee goes over to a big water tank that is located right by the house, turns a faucet on and drags a hose over to the burning house turns it on. Money starts to stream out of the end of the hose and smothers the house and puts the fire out.

3. Finally, I see myself sitting in my office and the assembly line of new employees is running by the office just out in the hall.

There you have it. Admittedly this is a fairly boring topic for most of us to talk about; however, using the memorization techniques that we've talked about you can see how you could "lock" this speech into your brain. When it came time to deliver the speech, all that you would have to do is sit back and play the stored images back on that big TV in your mind. What could be easier?

Chapter 4

Presentation Practice: How Much Is Enough?

Chapter 4: Presentation Practice: How Much Is Enough?

So you've got a big presentation / speech coming up. How many times should you practice your speech before you give it for real? This is actually a very good question that most presenters either forget to ask themselves or come up with the wrong answer to.

We all know that practice makes perfect so how can we tell when we've reached perfection with our speech?

We should probably start with the good news: even a little practice will probably make you better than most presenters. I can't tell you how many times I've had to sit through a train-wreck of a presentation that clearly showed that the presenter had laid out some thoughts on paper, but had not taken the time to practice what he/she was going to say.

If you want to create and deliver a great presentation, there are three key interlocked factors that you need to make sure that you take care of:

1. Make sure that the speech plays to your speaking strengths. If you hate to give speeches, make sure that this one is as short as possible in order to minimize your time "on stage". If you are good at telling stories, then include them in your presentation.

2. Establish good connections between the different parts of the speech. Ensuring that the speech flows smoothly and logically from section to section will make it much easier for you to memorize the flow of the speech.

3. Make sure that you have your speech down cold before you deliver it. You'll know that you've been able to do

this when you could recite it by heart if someone asked you to do so at a moment's notice. This will ensure that when you deliver your presentation the words tumble out of your mouth automatically and with no effort.

I'm not sure if you really want to hear this, but you cannot over-rehearse a presentation. I know that you are dying for a hard number to hang your hat on so here it is: 7.

I firmly believe that any presentation that you are going to deliver deserves at least seven practice runs by you. The first will be a flaming disaster and the seventh should be quite good.

This means that your "for real" presentation will be (at least) the 8th time that you've delivered the material and it should flow from you quite naturally. Key point: if this is one of those career defining presentations then you should probably practice it at least 15 times in order to make sure that each and every word comes out perfectly.

So we've answered the question of "how many" times you should practice, now the follow on question is "how to practice". The key to the first few run-throughs is to make sure that you are in a secure environment in which you won't be interrupted.

For most of us, this means a bathroom that has a lock on the door. The added advantage of practicing in a bathroom is that there is a large mirror in front of you and you can watch yourself as you talk. I can assure you that it's hard to do, but you'll eliminate unnecessary moves and twitches quickly when you practice this way.

Beginning speakers often want to make their presentation "perfect". This means that when they are practicing, they will speak until they screw-up, grit their teeth and then go back to the beginning and start over. This ensures that it's going to be hours before they can make it through the entire speech.

I recommend a different approach: start at the beginning and just run though the entire speech until you hit the end. Yes, there will be screw-ups; however, just keep on going.

Doing it this way will allow you to get a feel for the speech as a whole and you may end up changing big parts of it – no need to perfect something that you're going to be changing anyway.

Last point: get feedback. If the first time that you get feedback is when you present to your "real" audience than you've made a mistake. I can't begin to tell you just how important it is to get feedback from real humans as you prepare a presentation.

Words and ideas that seem to flow together for you may turn out to be confusing gibberish to them. Your cutting and trimming to make your speech fit in the allotted time may have caused you to skip over important definitions and concepts that are critical to your audience's understanding of your main points. It does not matter if the feedback comes from family, friends, strangers, or co-workers, just make sure that you get it.

Chapter 5

Lights, Camera, TV Presentation? 4 Tips For Speaking On Television

Chapter 5: Lights, Camera, TV Presentation? 4 Tips For Speaking On Television

Perhaps you have managed to overcome your fear of speaking to groups of people. Maybe you even have developed ways to deal with difficult questions and keep a presentation on track no matter what happens while you are speaking.

However, are you ready to take your skills to that ultimate broadcast medium – television? Probably not. There the rules are all different. It turns out that there are four simple things that you can do to make sure that you shine on the "boob tube".

Jo Jo Harder is a fashion designer who found herself being asked to appear on television shows after she started her "America's Top Dog Model" contest. Talk about being unprepared! Through her struggles and learning she has come up with four top tips for how a presenter should prepare to appear on television. Here they are:

1. **Know Your Subject & Be Prepared To Talk About It:** So this sounds sort of silly, but in the end it's really the reason that you are on television in the first place – you are the expert.

    One thing that you need to understand about television is that it's all about time management: you need to speak in short, crisp statements that leave an impression. Your time on camera will be very short and knowing your stuff will help you to make the most of it.

    I'm hoping that it goes without saying that you should spend some serious time practicing answering probable questions.

2. **Study Your Customer – The TV Show:** Even if you've never seen the show that you are going to be appearing on before, you had better spend some time coming up to speed on it.

   You need to know the names of the hosts, the name of the show's producer, and of course the basic format of the show. You need to know EVERYTHING that you can find out about the show including what time of day it is on, how long it's been on the air, where taping is going to be taking place.

   Of course, you also need to know WHAT you are expected to be talking about and just how long you will be expected to be speaking.

3. **Looks Count (A Lot!):** No matter what your mom told when you were growing up, on TV looks really do count for a lot.

   It's not so much about your looks (you look maaavvolous darling), but rather it's all about the clothes that you choose to wear. What you want to wear are bright, rich colors.

   What Harder recommends that we stay away from are white, ivory, and pastels with the exception of women's blouses and men's shirts worn under a jacket. Hopefully it goes without saying that EVERYONE needs to stay from bold prints, plaids, and check patterns.

   If you show up early enough and have a pleasant personality, you just might be able to get some attention from the show's makeup artist. This can be critical because without some help, we all have a bad habit of looking "washed out" under bright lights. Now just make sure that you've combed the hair and trimmed the nails and you should be good to go!

4. **Maintain Your Cool:** Remember that television is all about ratings and so the show is having you on in order to try to boost their ratings.

    That means that anything can happen ("That's interesting, but let me now introduce your long lost father...!"). Sit with your hands in your lap, your feet crossed away from the camera and look into the eyes of the person who is interviewing you.

    Smile as much as you can without seeming too weird. Help the show to manage its time by keeping your answers short and to the point. Always be prepared for the host to do something unusual and keep your cool at all times.

Chapter 6

Are You Acting Like A Presenter?

Chapter 6: Are You Acting Like A Presenter?

When you are asked to deliver a presentation, one way of looking at this request is that you are actually being asked to put on a one-person show. No matter if you are presenting at a college graduation or are simply reviewing last quarter's sales figures, you are an actor who is there to put on a show for your audience. Do you know how to act?

Ed Brodow is a professional speaker who has also spent 12 years as a Hollywood actor. Needless to say, he know his stuff. He points out that the actors that we like to watch on the big screen or on TV were not born that way. They've studied their craft and that's how they have become so good.

Brodow has worked with a number of acting coaches and he's discovered the acting skills that speakers need to incorporate into our presentations in order to make them more memorable. No, you're probably not going to win any Academy Awards for you next presentation; however, you might just do a better job of connecting with your audience.

Learn To Improvise: If you've delivered your presentation before or if you've spent the last month preparing for this presentation, then there is a chance that you are going to come across as "wooden" or "scripted". Having the ability to improvise, or make it up as you go along, is the key to making your presentation fresh and making the audience feel as though you make it up just for them.

Stories That Are Personal: We've talked about this before, but what makes any presentation memorable are your stories. Brodow reveals that the way an actor prepares for a scene with powerful emotions is to think back over their life and find a situation in which they were experiencing those emotions. They then substitute the scene that they are playing for their remembered scene and that's how they are able to convey such powerful emotions.

When you are presenting, don't just TELL a story. Instead, FEEL a story as you tell it. You audience will pick up on this and your stories will come alive for them.

What's Your Drive?: This is one of my biggest complaints about so many presentations that I've sat through – the speaker didn't have a point to make. When you present you need to have a single point – what are you advocating that the audience should do after you are done? How are you hoping to change them? If you don't have this, then you are just delivering a book report. Pick your position and then tell you audience why it's the right position for them also.

Be An Actor: Look, real life is rather boring – we see / live it every day. When you are presenting, you need to step-it-up-a-notch. You need to throw some drama into your words. You need to make your audience laugh. You need to stop being yourself and become an actor playing a role. Become larger than life and you will be able to put on a heck of a show for your audience.

Manage Your Energy: You are leading the show and so you need to be operating at a high level of energy. However, you also need to match you audience's energy level – if they are to low (like if you were talking to bankers these days) and you are too high, then you'll never connect to them. Instead, you need to sense their energy level and then start your presentation at an energy level that is just a bit higher than theirs. This way you'll connect with them and they'll follow you to whatever energy level you want to take them to.

There you go – this is a start. Anyone can stand before a group of people and deliver a boring presentation. In order to deliver a great presentation that will have an impact and will be memorable you need to become an actor!

Chapter 7

Why Don't You Act Like A Presenter During Your Presentation?

Chapter 7: Why Don't You Act Like A Presenter During Your Presentation?

Previously we had discussed the fact that any presentation that you give is really sort of like a one person show – if you know how to act, then you'll be more effective.

The challenge, of course, is that very few of us have been trained to be an actor. Additionally, we tend to think of actors as being "over the top" types of performers (sorta like Heath Leger in that Batman movie).

The truth is actually much different – acting is simply knowing what to say or how to move in order to influence your audience in some way. We'd all like to be able to do that, right?

Here are five acting tips that you can start using in order to improve your next presentation.

Speak In The Moment: In order to make your presentation more powerful, you need to fine tune it to your audience and their current mood. Great actors don't just memorize their lines, they "stay in the moment" and are constantly reacting to what's going on in their scene. You need to be constantly reacting to your audience's feedback and using this to modify how you present your information.

Keep It Fresh: There is the old saying that "variety is the spice of life". This is especially true when it comes to presentations. Anything that you do for too long will start to bore your audience. Today's audiences have very short attention spans and you need to be constantly changing your presentation in order to keep them engaged. Ways to change your presentation include emphasis, movement, volume, energy level or the material being presented.

Risky Business: If you are not taking any risks in your presentations, then you are not providing a dynamic presentation – it's going to be the same every time and that's boring. Trying out new things, interacting with audience members, these are all things that carry an element of risk. Risk keeps things interesting for both you and your audience.

Don't Be Afraid Of Commitment: When you decide to add some acting to your presentation, do it full throttle. The worst thing that you can do is go at it half speed. It's your passion and your commitment that will win your audience over in the end.

Concentration Is The Key To Relaxation: If you aren't careful and you let your mind wander, then you will end up focusing on just how nervous you are. Do what actors do: focus your mind on how you have prepared, the words that you want to say, and your audience – basically anything but your nerves.

There you have it, all of the tips that you need in order to start using the skills that actors use in your next presentation. I can't promise that you'll bring home a golden globe award, but the greatest complement will be if your audience can't wait to see your next show!

Chapter 8

The Presenter Super Memory System – An Overview

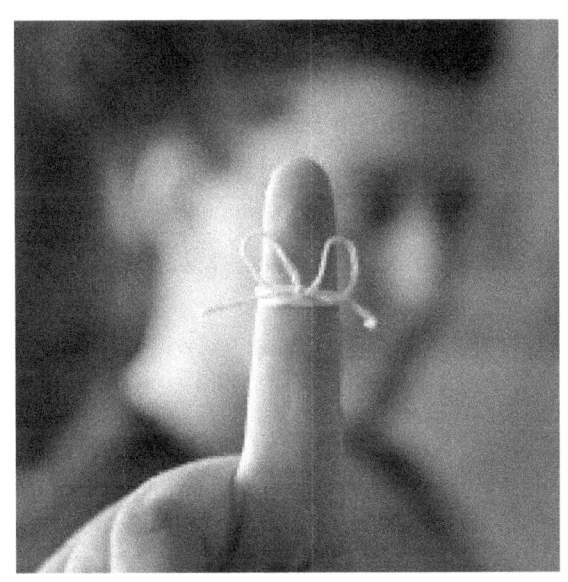

Chapter 8: The Presenter Super Memory System – An Overview

Congratulations – you've been invited to speak for 30 minutes. Remember – don't use any notes! If you got this offer could you do it?

As though standing in front of a group of people was not scary enough, now you have to find a way to shove 30 minutes (that's 1,800 seconds) worth of information into your head – and recall it under pressure. Given that we all talk at about 150 words/min, you're looking at **memorizing 4,500 words**. Good luck!

I recently had an opportunity to deliver a 45-minute keynote as part of a training session kick-off for a group of IT Managers. I decided that in order to boost my creditability with this hard-nosed group, I needed to stay in eye contact with them and not be looking at my notes. This meant memorization.

Now let me make a confession – **I hate it when people memorize their speeches**. When they do this, they have a tendency to deliver them in an automatic robot-like manner that has virtually no emotion because they are trying so hard to remember what they want to say next. I was determined to avoid this!

Here's what I did to get ready for this speech:

- I wrote the speech out word-for-word. This allowed me to create a 6,750 word speech (45 minutes) so that I would exactly fill my time slot.

- I then "tuned" the words trying to drop in as many memorable phrases into my speech as possible. This is the real advantage of writing your speech out completely.

- I then memorized the speech.

… and that's what you really want to do in order to memorize your speech. But, I'm out of space for now so I'll share all of the secrets about how I memorized this speech in the next Chapter…

Chapter 9

The Presenter Super Memory System – The Details

Chapter 9: The Presenter Super Memory System – The Details

I recently had an opportunity to deliver a 45-minute keynote as part of a training session kick-off for a group of IT Managers. I decided that in order to boost my creditability with this hard-nosed group, I needed to stay in eye contact with them and not be looking at my notes. This meant memorization.

Here's how I did it:

- I broke the speech up into sections – my speech resulted in 9 sections.

- I then broke each section up into "ideas" – basically sentences.

- I then picked a place that I had lived in the past (a school or any place that you know well would have done fine also). The only requirement was that it had to have multiple, distinct "locations" – in this case rooms.

- Then I pictured myself in a room such as the kitchen. I could see myself sitting at a table in a particular chair.

- Next I came up with a picture AND an action for the first idea / sentence that I wanted to memorize and I placed each image in a different spot in the kitchen.

Here's how I had written my speech to start out:

"I'd like to start out our time together today by asking you a simple question: where do you want you want to be at in your career 5 years from now? That will be 2020 – it's just 1,825 days from right now. I have no idea what you will be doing in 5 years, but there is one thing that I know with 100% certainty – the job that you are doing right now will no longer exist."

I basically had three image / actions to create. I was able to recall them by pretending that I was sitting in the kitchen and was looking around the room. Remember, these are highly personal – what you come up with just has to work for you.

- My first image was of 5 calendars: one each being stuck to each of the fingers on my right hand. I was shaking that hand very hard and they all flew off.

- My second image was of a stack of those one-a-day calendar tear-off sheets in a really, really tall pile sitting before me. Just to make it more vivid I pictured it as being sheets from the Dilbert: Day-to-Day Calendar. I then pictured a card in front of this stack that said "1,825 days" and the stack falling over and making a real mess on the floor.

- Finally, on the table in front of me behind the stack of calendar sheets was a very small model of a worker in a cubicle typing away on a computer. All of a sudden a trap door built into the table swung open and the little cubicle vanished.

There you have it. When I went to give my speech, I didn't even try to recall the words that I had written down. Instead, I had three pictures flash in sequence in my head – calendars stuck to my fingers, a stack of calendar pages, and a disappearing cubicle. Without looking at any notes, I was able to quickly and easily recall what I wanted to say without having to look at any notes!

Chapter 10

Hey Speaker – It's Tool Time!

Chapter 10: Hey Speaker – It's Tool Time!

When you find yourself giving a speech, you quickly realize that what you are missing is any sort of tools with which to give the speech. If you were a painter, you'd have a canvas, brushes, paints, thinners, etc. with which to make your creation. However, when you are giving a speech it's just you and your audience. Make you feel sorta naked, doesn't it?

It turns out that you actually do have a toolbox with which to create your speech – the words that you'll be using. It turns out that not only the words that you choose to use, but the way in which you speak these words can cause a powerful reaction in your audience. Debra Johanyak is a professor of English at the University of Akron and she has come up with a list of different ways that we can use our voice to make our point during a speech.

Let's take a look at the different verbal delivery "tools" that Dr. Johanyak has come up with:

- **Words That You Accent**: It turns out that not all words are created equal – you have the ability to emphasize certain words. As an example, consider the sentence *"After cutting the green wire, a sudden silence descended over the entire bomb squad."* Simply by pronouncing the word "green" differently, you can draw your audience's attention to it.

- **Slow Pitch Speaking:** The pitch of your voice controls how high and how low your voice goes. This is a powerful way to communicate emotion during your speech: "Once I saw that the cage was empty, I knew that the 6' snake could be *anywhere* in the house." The word "anywhere" can be said in a higher pitch than the other words in order to draw attention to it.

- **Just Be Quiet**: The most powerful speaking tool is also the simplest – just be quiet. When we add periods of silence to our speeches, it adds emphasis to the words that came before and sets the stage for the words that are to come next.

There you have it – now your speaking toolbox is actually looking rather full!

Chapter 11

Your Presentation Voice: Is That Really Me?

Chapter 11: Your Presentation Voice: Is That Really Me?

We've all had that moment of disbelief – you know the one, when someone recorded you saying something and then played it back to you. You listened to the voice coming out of the speaker and you did what we all do – you winced and said "**No way that's me!**" However, yes it was you – as you sound to everyone but yourself. Ouch!

From that moment on, you were forever changed. Just like in that move "The Matrix", you had taken the red pill and now you couldn't ever turn back – you now know **how your voice sounds to others**.

Nancy Meyer is a national speaker and author who has spent a lot of time looking into why we sound different to ourselves than we do to others. I think that **she's solved this mystery**.

Nancy says that the reason that we sound so different to ourselves has **three reasons**: your inner ear, your outer ear, and where your voice comes from. Of course, that's not quite enough info for you to do anything about it. So let's dive in just a bit deeper and find out what all of this means.

- **Your Inner Ear:** Your speaking voice originates in the middle of your neck. You expel air which then passes through your vocal cords, gets magnified in your voice box, resonates in the cavities in your head and then the sound exits out your nose and / or mouth. Your inner ear (the part that actually "hears" sounds) is located quite close to all of this so only you get to hear your voice as it starts out.

- **Your Outer Ear:** So here's something that you may not have thought of – you don't actually hear the sounds coming out of your mouth. If you think about this, your ears are in the wrong place to hear what's coming out of your mouth. Instead, what happens is that the sounds that come out of your mouth shoot out, bounce off of something, and then get picked up by your ears. This means that what you are actually hearing is really the sound of your voice plus a lot of extra noises.

- **Where Your Voice Comes From:** Since you are creating the sounds that you speak in your throat, these vibrations end up rattling your entire head. This means that the parts of your ear that pick up sound are getting bounced around just by the very fact that you are speaking. This changes what you hear.

So this all leads to the big question: what if **you don't like** the voice that others are hearing coming out of your mouth? In all honesty, there's not a lot that you can do.

The key recommendation is that you **don't change your voice drastically** – small changes are the best. You can practice with a tape recorder making changes and then playing them back. If you still don't like what you are hearing then it may be time to go out and invest in a vocal coach. You should hear what you've been missing!

Chapter 12

This Speech Will Be Delivered In (Good) English

Chapter 12: This Speech Will Be Delivered In (Good) English

I've always spoken English. I never really spent a lot of time thinking about what it took to speak **"good English"** because it's my native tongue.

However, when I started working with speakers for whom English was not their first language, I quickly came to understand just how hard it is to give a good speech in English if it's not your first language. That's "hard", but not "impossible"…

The Challenge Of Speaking In English As A Second Language

While working with clients, I've often been asked "so how can I improve my English speaking skills?" The people asking me this are generally well-educated and do an ok job of speaking English in personal conversations, it's just when it comes to giving a speech **that things seem to fall apart for them**.

I always have to break it to them that there is no **magic "silver bullet"** to improving one's English. So much of the language is based less on the words themselves and rather on how the words are used. Given this limitation, I offer them the following three suggestions:

1. **Dive In:** the best way to pick up on how any language is being used in real life is to immerse yourself in it as much as you can. This means that you need to break out of your circle of friends who speak your native language and spend more time with English speakers. No it's not going to be easy, but this is one of the best ways to learn.

2. **Read, read, read**: I'm not talking about spending time with the classics of English literature, but rather taking the time to read the daily newspaper and weekly magazines (USA Today, Time, People, Rolling Stone, etc.). These media sources are written to be read by the masses and by studying how they communicate, you'll both build your vocabulary and you'll shape how you use your words.

3. **Get A Role Model**: there's got to be someone in your life that you believe does a very good job of speaking English. TV personalities are just fine for this task. Spend the time studying them, repeat what they say, and work to "become" them. This will not only improve your English language skills, but it will also give you the confidence that you'll need the next time you are giving a speech.

Ways To Hide Any English Problems That You May Have

English is a goofy language. It has been built from so many other languages that it can be very difficult to master. Since it will take time to improve your English speaking skills, one of the things that you can do right away is to change how you give a speech in order to hide any English challenges that you are having.

The first thing that you can do is to start to use more one-syllable words. All too often I see my clients attempting to use complex multi-syllable words in order to impress their audience; however, since these words can be harder to pronounce correctly they just end up taking away from the impact of their speech. Using short words gives your speech a "punch" that will connect with your audience.

Next, you need to keep your sentences short. All too often non-native English speakers tend to create long and involved sentences that just seem to go on and on. The right thing to do is after you've created a speech take the time to go back and break-up any long thoughts into multiple short thoughts. This way you'll be able to speak more clearly and connect with your audience better.

Ways To Improve The English That You Use In Your Speeches

There are several things that a non-native English speaker can do to improve a speech. Once again, these are probably best introduced over time as the speaker becomes more comfortable with using them:

- **Stories Are Good**: every audience loves a good story. Taking the time to build a story that paints a vivid mental image will capture your audience's imagination and will allow them to overlook any language issues.

- **Incorporate Places**: the more that you can include places that your audience can visualize, the easier it will be for them to follow your speech. If you stumble over some words, it won't matter because your audience is already picturing what you are talking about.

What All Of This Means For You

English is a fantastic language – so much can be expressed in it. However, it is among the most difficult of languages to learn. Learning to apply what you've learned about another language when you are delivering a speech in English is hard to do, but the results make it well worth the effort!

It's from the forge of failure that the steel of success is formed.

Hard Work Does Not Guarantee Success, But Success Does Not Happen Without Hard Work.

- Dr. Jim Anderson

Create Speeches That Motivate Your Audiences And Get Your Message Heard!

Dr. Jim Anderson is available to provide training and coaching on the topics that are the most important to people who have to speak in public: how can I create a speech that people want to hear and how can I deliver in a way that will allow me to connect with my audience and get my point across to them?

Dr. Anderson believes that in order to both learn and remember what he says, speakers need to laugh. Each one of his speeches is full of fun and humor so that what he says "sticks" with everyone.

Dr. Anderson's Public Speaking Training Includes:

1. How to plan your next speech: pick your purpose and understand your audience.
2. What's the best way to get PowerPoint and Keynote to work with you, not against you?
3. What do you need to do when you are presenting in order to truly connect with your audience?

Dr. Jim Anderson presents over 100 speeches per year. To invite Dr. Anderson to speak at your event, contact him at: **Phone: 813-418-6970** or **Email:** jim@BlueElephantConsulting.com

Photo Credits:

Cover - By: Geert Hofman
http://www.flickr.com/photos/31339239@N07/

Chapter 1 - By: Josh DiMauro
http://www.flickr.com/photos/jazzmasterson/

Chapter 2 - By: Thomas Hawk
http://www.flickr.com/photos/thomashawk/

Chapter 3 - By: Quinn Dombrowski
http://www.flickr.com/photos/quinnanya/

Chapter 4 - By: Christine
http://www.flickr.com/photos/bigpinkcookie/

Chapter 5 - By: Peter Dutton
http://www.flickr.com/photos/joeshlabotnik/

Chapter 6 - By: John
http://www.flickr.com/photos/mtsofan/

Chapter 7 - By: Vancouver Film School
http://www.flickr.com/photos/vancouverfilmschool/

Chapter 8 - By: Flood G.
http://www.flickr.com/photos/_flood_/

Chapter 9 - By: John Morris
http://www.flickr.com/photos/jm999uk/

Chapter 10 - By: Daniel Brock
http://www.flickr.com/photos/brockamer/

Chapter 11 - By: Carbon Arc
http://www.flickr.com/photos/41002268@N03/

Chapter 12 - By: Kheel Center
http://www.flickr.com/photos/kheelcenter/

Other Books By The Author

Product Management

- How To Have A Successful Product Manager Career: The Things That You Need To Be Doing TODAY In Order To Have A Successful Product Manager Career

- Product Manager Product Success: How to keep your product on track and make it become a success

- Communication Skills For Product Managers: The Communication Skills That Product Managers Need To Know How To Use In Order To Have A Successful Product

- Customer Lessons For Product Managers: Techniques For Product Managers To Better Understand What Their Customers Really Want

Public Speaking

- Secrets To Planning The Perfect Speech

- Secrets To Organizing The Perfect Speech: How to organize the best speech of your life!

- Secrets To Creating The Perfect Speech: How to create a speech that will make your message be remembered forever!

- How To Rehearse In Order To Give The Perfect Speech: How to effectively rehearse your next speech to that your message be remembered forever!

CIO Skills

- CIO Business Skills: How CIOs can work effectively with the rest of the company!

- Managing Your CIO Career: Steps That CIOs Have To Take In Order To Have A Long And Successful Career

- CIO Communication Skills Secrets: Tips And Techniques For CIOs To Use In Order To Become Better Communicators

- How CIOs Can Make Innovation Happen: Tips And Techniques For CIOs To Use In Order To Make Innovation Happen In Their IT Department

IT Manager Skills

- IT Manager Budgeting Skills

- IT Manager Career Secrets: Tips And Techniques That IT Managers Can Use In Order To Have A Successful Career

- Secrets Of Effective Leadership For IT Managers : Tips And Techniques That IT Managers Can Use In Order To Develop Leadership Skills

Negotiating

- Preparing For Your Next Negotiation: What You Need To Do BEFORE A Negotiation Starts In Order To Get The Best Possible Deal

- How To Open Your Next Negotiation: How To Start A Negotiation In Order To Get The Best Possible Outcome

Miscellaneous

- Power Distribution Unit (PDU) Secrets: What Everyone Who Works In A Data Center Needs To Know!

- Making The Jump: How To Land Your Dream Job When You Get Out Of College!

"How to effectively rehearse your next speech so that your message will be remembered forever!"

> This book has been written with one goal in mind – to show you how you can rehearse your next speech so that it will be a success. We're going to show you what you need to be doing in order to memorize and present a great speech!
>
> **Let's Make Your Next Speech A Success!**

What You'll Find Inside:

- **HOW TO USE YOUR MENTAL TV TO MEMORIZE A SPEECH (OR ANYTHING)**

- **PRESENTATION PRACTICE: HOW MUCH IS ENOUGH?**

- **LIGHTS, CAMERA, TV PRESENTATION? 4 TIPS FOR SPEAKING ON TELEVISION**

- **YOUR PRESENTATION VOICE: IS THAT REALLY ME?**

Dr. Jim Anderson brings his 25 years of real-world experience to this book. He's delivered speeches at some of the world's largest firms as well as at many conferences. He's going to show you what you need to do in order to make your next speech a success!

www.ingramcontent.com/pod-product-compliance
Lightning Source LLC
Chambersburg PA
CBHW071808170526
45167CB00003B/1227